the Quotable

"I Love Lucy"®

MetroBooks

An Imprint of Friedman/Fairfax Publishers

This edition published by Metrobooks by
arrangement with Quirk Productions, Inc.

Printed in Singapore
Designed by Simone Kane
Quotations compiled by Stephanie Chizek

A Quirk Book
www.quirkproductions.com

ISBN 1-58663-288-4

1 3 5 7 9 10 8 6 4 2

For bulk purchases and special sales,
please contact:

Friedman/Fairfax Publishers
Attention: Sales Department
15 West 26th Street
New York, NY 10010
212/685-6610 FAX 212/685-1307

Visit our website:
www.metrobooks.com

the Quotable

"I Love Lucy"®

MetroBooks

Contents

"Ever since we said 'I do,' there are so many things **we don't.**"

Introduction

This statement was first uttered by Lucy Ricardo in the premiere telecast of I Love Lucy® **on October 15, 1951. And in the fifty years since then,** I Love Lucy® **has entertained millions of people around the world, while making an undeniable impact on the history and evolution of television sitcoms.**

Critics have always applauded the talents of Lucy, Ricky, Fred, and Ethel (also known as Lucille Ball, Desi Arnaz, William Frawley, and Vivian Vance). More recently, however, fans and scholars have come to appreciate the vast contributions of the show's writers. Lucille Ball herself led the way: "I am nothing without my writers," she admitted on many occasions. "I don't think funny. But I am pretty good at interpreting the things my writers dream up for me." Pretty good, indeed.

The people doing the "dreaming up" on I Love Lucy® were Jess Oppenheimer, Bob Carroll, Jr., Madelyn Pugh, Bob Weiskopf, and Bob Schiller. (Carroll and Pugh were with the show its entire 1951–1957 run; Oppenheimer served as producer and head writer the first five years; Weiskopf and Schiller joined the show in 1955.)

All five writers had had extensive experience in radio. Oppenheimer, Carroll, and Pugh wrote for Lucy's radio show, "My Favorite Husband," and had a keen ear for "middle American vernacular." Perhaps more important, they also had a knack for writing scenes that were visually funny—even on radio. Lucy often praised her radio scribes for creating material for "Husband" that was more visually interesting than many of the scripts she was being sent by Hollywood movie producers. No wonder she brought them along when she made the transition to television!

As I Love Lucy® would prove, Oppenheimer and Company were masters of verbal humor as well. Not the kind of "line, line, joke; line, line, joke" humor often found in vaudeville (and TV variety show) sketches, but honest, character-driven humor that evolved naturally out of a given situation. I Love Lucy® story lines often reflected the mood and desires of post-war middle-class America: It was a time of rampant consumerism, in which "keeping up with the Joneses" became something of an art-form; a time when new affluence allowed for cross-country and overseas travel; and a time when big city life was often given up for more spacious living in the suburbs. Lucy tackled all of these trends beautifully.

Whatever the plot, the series was first and foremost a love story between two people who clearly adored each other, and between two sets of friends who remained loyal through thick and through thin. Ironically, the writers chose to underscore this devotion not with sappy on-screen dialogue, but usually with rather sarcastic remarks. For example, in one episode we find this exchange:

RICKY:

I'm just gonna tell Sam exactly the way I think about marriage.

LUCY:

Don't you dare!

In another, there's this:

ETHEL:

He should have more consideration. After all, I gave him the best years of my life.

FRED:

Were those the best?

And finally, this:

LUCY:

Oh, gee, Ethel, thanks. . . . It's times like these when you know what friends are for.

ETHEL:

If I'd known this is what friends are for, I'd have signed up as an enemy.

Still other classic Lucy lines are veritable word games. When Lucy and Ricky select names for their soon-to-be-born child, they quickly rule out "John" and "Mary." "Mary's all right," explains Lucy, "but every Tom, Dick and Harry's named John." In the same episode she says, "I want the names to be unique and euphonious." "Okay," agrees Ricky. " 'Unique' if it's a boy, and 'Euphonious' if it's a girl!"

We could go on and on citing wonderful lines—and, in fact, we will! What follows is a collection of the all-time-greatest Lucy quotes, culled from all 180 half-hour episodes of *I Love Lucy*®. The list does not pretend to be exhaustive—that would require several volumes the size of the Oxford English Dictionary—but many favorites are here. We have divided them thematically, but all have two things in common: each is bound to evoke a memory and is guaranteed to make you smile. Enjoy!

—Tom Watson, President
We Love Lucy Fan Club

Love and Marriage

LUCY:

Husbands make me so mad. They're always promising you they'll do something for you and then they don't do it.

ETHEL:

Well, that's one problem I never have with Fred.

LUCY:

You don't?

ETHEL:

Nope, he never promises to do anything for me in the first place.

LUCY:

I love you.

RICKY:

Lucy, what do you want?

RICKY:

Hey listen, do you know anything about rice?

FRED:

Well, I had it thrown at me on one of the darkest days of my life.

RICKY:

After all, if this guy is fortunate enough to still be single—

LUCY:

What?

RICKY:

I didn't mean it that way. I mean, if he's smart enough to still be single—

LUCY:

How's that?

RICKY:

There must be some word that describes what I'm trying to say.

LUCY:

The word is stupid.

RICKY:

All right. Stupid. If the guy's stupid enough to still be single, leave him alone.

LUCY:

That's better.

RICKY:

After all, ignorance is bliss.

LUCY:

Now, what would you do if the first time I met you, I insulted you, spilled stuff all over you, and acted like a first class nincompoop?

RICKY:

Just what I did: wait for my suit to come back from the cleaners, then marry you.

LUCY:

Dishwater is very hard on diamond rings.

RICKY:

When we got married, you said you would never take your ring off.

LUCY:

When we got married, you said that dishwater would never touch these lily-white hands!

LUCY:
Is Ethel there?

FRED:
No.

LUCY:
Well, where is she?

FRED:
How should I know?

LUCY:
Well, she's your wife.

FRED:
Did you wake me
up just to rub it in?

FRED:

Eventually, every married woman gets the feeling that her husband wants to kill her. And she's usually right.

RICKY:
Look, Lucy. This whole
thing was my fault.

LUCY:
Your fault?

RICKY:
It was something that I said
that started this whole thing.

LUCY:
What did you say?

RICKY:
"I do."

RICKY:

Listen Fred, I got an awful problem on my hands.

FRED:

You should have thought of that before you married her!

LUCY:
Oh, I'll hang that up for you, dear.

RICKY:
I can do it, honey.

LUCY:
No, no, no, honey. That's what wives are for.

FRED:
Oh, so that's what they're for.

DR. PETERSON:
I'm the doctor that brought your wife into the world.

RICKY:
Well, I don't know whether to thank you or punch you in the nose.

LUCY:
Ricky is giving me something.
Something that every woman has
always wanted from her husband.

ETHEL:
A divorce?

ETHEL:
Ricky and Fred
are cut out of the
same mold.

LUCY:
Yeah, and they're
getting moldier.

ETHEL:

My woman's club wants Ricky.

· ·

LUCY:

Well, I'd be very happy to help them out, but I'm not through with him yet.

LUCY:
For fourteen years Ricky's been
trusting, devoted, understanding.
And what have I been? Thoughtless,
selfish, meddlesome, bungling,
scheming, conniving, ehhh . . .

FRED:
Irritating, headstrong, obnoxious—

ETHEL:

Fred!

LUCY:
It's all right, Ethel.
Let him alone. He's right.

ETHEL:
Well, as long as it's
open season, how about

petty, childish,
stubborn, vain—

LUCY:
All right, let's not get
carried away!

LUCY:

Now, honey, remember when we were married you wanted to be joined together in matrimony.

RICKY:

And as I recall it was "'til death do us part."

LUCY:

Yeah, that's right.

RICKY:

Well, that event is about to take place right now!

Money

FRED:

Say, is that Lucy
Ricardo? May I have
your autograph?

LUCY:

Oh, Fred, don't be smart.

FRED:

Who's being smart?
I want it on a check for
this month's rent.

LUCY:

Budget my time? You mean, like I budget my money?

RICKY:

Heaven forbid!

LUCY:

This is my system for paying bills. You see, I throw them all up in the air and the ones that land face up are the winners.

ETHEL:

By "the winners" you mean the ones you pay?

LUCY:

Uh-huh.

ETHEL:

But what happens if they all land face up?

LUCY:

Well, then I just switch: I only pay the ones that lay face down.

RICKY:

Do you realize how many times I'm going to have to sing "Babalu" to pay for that house?

LUCY:

Well, maybe there is no profit on each individual jar, but we'll make it up in volume.

RICKY:

How much does it cost to make?

LUCY:

Oh, uh . . .

ETHEL:

Oh, uh . . .

LUCY:

Well, we didn't figure that.

RICKY:

Well, what did you figure?

LUCY:

Well, we figured that you just buy the oil and the onions and stuff and sell it and what's left over is profit.

RICKY:

And what if there's nothing left over?

LUCY:

Well, there's got to be something left over. How else can we make a million dollars?

FRED:
That engine is solid as a dollar.

RICKY:
Yeah, that's about all it's worth, too.

FRED:
We've got a few bucks set aside.

LUCY:
Oh? Have you, Ethel?

ETHEL:
Only every dollar we ever made!

LUCY:

You heard what Fred said: "possession is nine points of the law" and I'm possessed!

FRED:

Ethel tells me your faucet's leaking.

LUCY:

Well, you didn't have to rush over. I told her two years ago!

LUCY:

Wouldn't you feel terrible if you went home without seeing the queen?

ETHEL:

I'd feel much worse if I went home without spending the money Fred gave me.

LUCY:

I drew in an extra hour at the bottom of the chart.

ETHEL:

Where did you get the extra hour?

LUCY:

From the next day.

ETHEL:

From the next day?

LUCY:

Yeah. It'll work out fine until the end of the year, and then I'll be two weeks short.

LUCY:

A plain, simple, little dress like this—$500? I don't believe it.

ETHEL:

How are you going to explain the extra cost to Ricky?

LUCY:

I don't know. I don't know.

ETHEL:

Well, you can't take it back; it's been altered.

LUCY:

Yeah, and when Ricky finds out about it I'll be altered!

LUCY:

That's why they call them tellers. They go around blabbing everything they know.

FRED:
Two other people wanted to buy this car.

LUCY:
Where were they from, the Smithsonian Institute?

FRED:

Ethel, cancel our subscription.

ETHEL:

We don't take this paper.

FRED:

Well, order a subscription and then cancel it!

LUCY:

About a year and a half ago, Ricky wanted to go over my household account, and I was ten dollars short.

ETHEL:

So?

LUCY:

Well, I borrowed ten dollars from the club treasury so that my household account would balance.

ETHEL:

Well, ten dollars, my goodness.

LUCY:

Well, you don't understand, Ethel. That was only the beginning. From then on I borrowed from the household account so that the treasury would balance and then I borrowed from the treasury so the household account would balance and on and on and back and forth like a tennis game, and somewhere along the line I lost the ball.

ETHEL:

What do you mean?

LUCY:

Now there's no money in either account.

Show Business

LUCY:

Ricky! Ricky! I've asked you to let me be in that show before, but I've never meant it as much as I do this time. If you don't let me be in your show at the Palladium, I'm going to give you such a punch, you'll talk funnier than you do now!

RICKY:

Lucy, are you playing an F sharp?

LUCY:

Well, I'm not sure.

RICKY:

What do you mean you're not sure?

LUCY:

Well, are you talking about the fat little white note or the black one with the wiggly tail?

ETHEL:

Well, what are you going to do? Call up the studio and tell 'em you can't make it?

LUCY:

No, I can make it. I'll tell 'em Ricky can't make it.

ETHEL:

They won't want you without Ricky.

LUCY:

Why do you say that?

ETHEL:

Because it's the truth.

LUCY:

Well, I know, but why do you say it?

Hello, friends. I'm your Vitameatavegamin girl. Are you tired, run-down, listless? Do you poop out at parties? Are you unpopular? The answer to all your problems is in this little bottle. Yes, Vitameatavegamin. Vitameatavegamin contains vitamins, meat, vegetables and minerals. With Vitameatavegamin you can spoon your way to health. All you do is take a big tablespoonful after every meal. It's so tasty, too: it tastes just like candy. So why don't you join the thousands of happy, peppy people and buy a great big bottle of Vitameatavegamin tomorrow? That's Vitameatavegamin.

Well, I'm your Vita-vega-vittivat girl. Are you tired? Run-down? Listless? Do you pop out at parties? Are you unpoopular? Well, are you? The answer to all your problems is in this little ol' bottle. . . . Vitameatavegemin. That's it. Vitameatavegemin contains vitamins, meat, megetables and vinerals. So why don't you join the thousands of happy, peppy people and get a great big bottle of Vita-veaty-vega-meany-minie-moe-amin. I'll tell you what you have to do. You have to take a whole tablespoonful after every meal. It's so tasty, too; it's just like candy. So every-body get a bottle of . . . this stuff.

RICKY:

Look, honey. This is too big a chance for me. I need someone with a lot of 'sperience.

LUCY:

Well, I've had 'sperience.

RICKY:

You've never even been on a television show.

LUCY:

Well, maybe not, but I've watched 'em a lot.

LUCY:

Aw, Ricky, please. Just let me do the commercial.

RICKY:

Nothin' doing.

LUCY:

Why not?

ETHEL:
You're a very clever person.
You can do lots of things . . .

LUCY:
Such as?

ETHEL:
Well, you're just wonderful
at . . . uh . . . You've always
been tops, uh . . .

LUCY:
Those are the same ones
Ricky came up with.

ETHEL:

Isn't that a wonderful idea?

LUCY:

Well, no.
That way I don't get to sing alone.

ETHEL:

That's what makes it a
wonderful idea.

LUCY:

As a dancer,
I have two left feet,
and as a singer,
I sound like a bull
moose pulling his foot
out of the mud.

LUCY:

There are just two things keeping
me from dancing in that show.

FRED:

Your feet?

LUCY:

Listen, you haven't even heard them
play and you want them in the
orchestra. Why don't you want me?

ETHEL:

I've heard you play.

LUCY:

Gee, did you hear that, honey? It's going to be called **Bitter Grapes**. I wonder what part they want for me.

FRED:

Oh, you're probably going to be one of the bunch.

LUCY:

I was just trying to see
if I was real nearsighted,
if maybe you couldn't
pass for Marilyn Monroe.

ETHEL:

Yeah?

LUCY:

Yeah, pull your hair
down over one eye. . . .
Now walk like Marilyn. . . .
Ah, no.

Nobody's that nearsighted!

Language

RICKY:

Oooh! They're trying to make us look at this thing through a sweater!

LUCY:

Oh, you mean they're trying to pull the wool over our eyes!

LUCY:

I don't think that's very nice, making fun of my Spanish.

RICKY:

Well, you've been making fun of my English for fifteen years.

LUCY:

That's different. Spanish is a foreign language.

RICKY:

Well, English is a foreign language to me.

LUCY:

Well, the way you speak it, it is to me, too.

RICKY:
And that's an ultimatum!

LUCY:
An ultimatum?

ETHEL:
Well, I'm not surprised.

LUCY:
I am. I didn't think he
knew how to pronounce it.

LUCY:

Ethel, you know how your apartment is . . .

ETHEL:

What do you mean?

LUCY:

Well, the way it looks. Let's face it, it's sort of . . .
well, uh . . . What's the word I'm looking for?

ETHEL:

I don't use that kind of language.

FRED:
You don't suppose she's a
kleptomaniac?

RICKY:
No, I just think
she steals things.

RICKY:
How do you spell 'sperienced?

LUCY:
E-x-p—

RICKY:
E-x? You're kidding!

LUCY:

I want the names to be
unique and euphonious.

RICKY:

Okay, "Unique" if
its a boy, and "Euphonious"
if its a girl.

Friendship

LUCY (TO ETHEL):

Happy birthday, and I hope you live another seventy-five years!

RICKY:

I don't think it's a good idea to get too friendly with the neighbors too fast.

LUCY:

Why not? We're going to be living here the rest of our lives. Why shouldn't we get friendly with the neighbors right away?

RICKY:

That's just it. We are going to be here for the rest of our lives, so I think that we should get chummy gradually.

LUCY:

Oh, well maybe you can get chummy gradually. With me, it's instant chummy.

LUCY:

You've got to agree I'm better than nothing.

ETHEL:

There you've got me.

LUCY:

That must be my dear friend Ethel. Please, Fred, I'll open the door.

FRED:

Open it? I was going to lock it!

FRED:
The test of true friendship does not depend upon buying gifts.

ETHEL:
He oughta know. He's been testing his friends for twenty years.

FRED:
Who is it?

ETHEL:
It's Lucy and she's in trouble.

FRED:
Quick, hang up!

LUCY:

The last time we played bridge, you said you'd never want to play with me again.

What happened?

ETHEL:

Our television set's broken.

LUCY:
Oh, gee, Ethel, thanks.
It's times like these when you
know what friends are for.

ETHEL:
If I'd known this was
what friends were for,
I'd have signed up as an
enemy!

The Battle of the Sexes

ETHEL:
Are you insinuating that
I'm daft, loony, off my
rocker, out of my head?

FRED:
Well, that covers it
pretty well.

LUCY:

Now you never know. Before the evening is through we may see a spook.

RICKY:

Don't tell me you invited your mother!

RICKY:

I'm just so upset, I don't know what I'm doing.

FRED:

Now what's Lucy done?

RICKY:

A few truthful criticisms will do us all a lot of good.

ETHEL:

Oh, that's easy for you to say. She hasn't said anything about you yet.

RICKY:

OK, go ahead, Lucy, tell me my faults. Tell me what you really think of me.

LUCY:

I think you are the most handsome, the most wonderful, the cleverest and the most talented man in the whole world.

RICKY:

The truth didn't hurt me.

ETHEL:

Oh, brother.

RICKY:

Can you think of any other faults of mine?

LUCY:

Yes, you're hammy, you're stubborn, and you're a coward.

LUCY:
You could forget
you ever knew me.

RICKY:
That's a very
tempting offer.

RICKY:
Maybe she has a sixth sense.

FRED:
She might. She never had any before.

ETHEL:
It's been years since
we sat in a movie
with your arm
around my waist.

FRED:
It's been years since
my arm reached
around your waist.

LUCY:

How would you feel if Fred were smoldering with jealousy?

ETHEL:

Fred wouldn't smolder if he backed into a blow-torch.

LUCY:
I don't know what
happened to Ethel!

FRED:
Well, let's just hope
for the best.

RICKY:
Don't worry, Fred.
She'll show up.

FRED:
I said let's hope for
the best.

LUCY:

You're such a
peso pincher.

ETHEL:

Where's Ricky?

LUCY:

**He went into New York.
How about Fred?**

ETHEL:

He's takin' a nap.

LUCY:

How do you know that?

ETHEL:

**It's after lunch and before
dinner. What else would he
be doing?**

ETHEL:

These Italian trains sure are cramped. Imagine: one seat for four people.

FRED:

She said my mother looks like a weasel!

LUCY:

Ethel, apologize!

ETHEL:

Fred, I'm sorry your mother looks like a weasel.

FRED:

Ethel, will you stop complaining?

ETHEL:

Well, it's true. They're not very roomy.

FRED:

They're roomy enough.
It's just that you're roomier.

FRED:

Now don't make fun of us doughboys.

ETHEL:

Doughboys?

LUCY:

Whoever put the dough in that boy used too much yeast.

LUCY:

If some woman was trying to take Fred away from you, you'd sing another tune.

ETHEL:

Yeah, "Happy Days Are Here Again!"

RICKY:

Now, honey, why don't you be a good girl? You don't hear Ethel asking Fred to buy her a new dress.

ETHEL:
If I lost my wedding ring we wouldn't have to find it. We'd just have to buy another box of Cracker Jack.

ETHEL:

I'll be lucky if he buys me my lunch.

ETHEL:
What's the matter?
Haven't you ever
seen me eat before?

FRED:
I've never seen you
do anything else!

Planning and Scheming

LUCY:
I didn't tell a soul,
and they all promised
to keep it a secret.

RICKY:

Now, just a minute. Everybody,
please, now. We have to concentrate.
We have to use our brains.

LUCY:

Well, now, let me see . . .

RICKY:

You stay out of this.

LUCY:
He'll listen to you, Ricky. You tell him that I have a wonderful plan that won't cost him a cent.

RICKY:
My scatterbrained wife has another half-witted scheme and if you listen to it you're out of your mind.

LUCY:
Boy, did I suffer in that translation.

LUCY:

Listen, you stall them until I can get that meat out of the freezer.

ETHEL:

How can I stall them?

LUCY:

Listen, Ethel, if I can move seven hundred pounds of meat, you oughta be able to keep two husbands occupied for a couple of minutes.

ETHEL:

What can I do?

LUCY:

Dance with them. Talk. Sing. That's it. Ask Ricky to sing.

ETHEL:

Sing? You know he won't.

LUCY:

Oh, won't he? Listen, you take care of the ham. I'll take care of the beef.

LUCY:
Hey, I've got an
idea! No, maybe
it's too wild.

ETHEL:
If you've got an
idea that you think
is too wild, I don't
want to hear it.

LUCY:

I have an idea!

ETHEL:

How can you stand there in the middle of all this mess and utter those four horrible words: "I've got an idea!"?

LUCY:
We've been in worse
jams than this. **ETHEL:**
Yes, thanks to you.

Beauty and Fashion

ETHEL:

Do you think they
could make a glamour
girl out of me?

LUCY:

Sure, it says right here:
"We work miracles."

ETHEL:

Oh, I don't think those Italian actresses are so much. Not one of them has got her hair combed.

FRED:

Well, they look great to me.

ETHEL:

If I let my hair go like that, you'd never let me hear the end of it.

FRED:

Honey bunch, if the rest of you looked like that I wouldn't care if you were bald.

RICKY:

Who knows what could happen?

FRED:

Yeah, with all that champagne, even Ethel might look good.

ETHEL:
I refuse to go to
the theater with
anyone who thinks
I'm a hippopotamus.

RICKY:
Did you call her
that?

LUCY:
All I did was intimate
that she was a little
hippy, but on second
glance she has got the
biggest potamus
I've ever seen.

ETHEL:

Really, honey, were you afraid you'd lose me?

FRED:

I'll say. That outfit you're wearing is RENTED.

ETHEL:

Come on, let me see your new dress!

LUCY:

All right, calm down. You're acting like you never saw a new dress before.

ETHEL:

Who's acting?

FRED:

Oh, brother, if
Ethel's trying to be
glamorous she won't
be ready for a week.

Growing Old

LUCY:

That house won't be ours for twenty years.

RICKY:

Now, honey. Now, now. There's nothing to cry about.

LUCY:

Oh no? I just figured out how old I'll be in twenty years!

WOMAN:

**What's the date of
your birthday?**

LUCY:

August sixth.

WOMAN:

August sixth what?

 **LUCY:**

**August sixth
period.**

RICKY:

Do you realize how old we will be in twenty years? I'll be fifty-six and you'll be—

LUCY:

Never mind.

RICKY:

Now, honey, I know how old you are.

LUCY:

I know, but I've been juggling my age for so many years I've kinda forgotten what it is and I want to leave it that way.

LUCY:

Yeah, he's pushing twenty-three all right. In fact, he's pushed it all the way to thirty-five.

RICKY:

As a matter of fact, how old are you now?

LUCY:

Sixty-five.

RICKY:

What do you think—I'm a dope or something? You couldn't possibly be sixty-five.

LUCY:

I couldn't?

RICKY:

Of course not. Look at you. Fifty-five yes, but not sixty-five.

RICKY:
Imagine that. A whole week off with nothing to do but just hang around the house.

FRED:
Yeah, I ought to take a week off myself sometime.

ETHEL:
From what? You've been hanging around the house for twenty-three years. I wish you'd take a week off and go someplace.

FRED:
Has it only been twenty-three years?

FRED:

What do you mean you want forty dollars for a lamp?

ETHEL:

What I said: we don't have a decent lamp to read by.

FRED:

Listen, Ethel. If you want to read, you can read by firelight. If it was good enough for Abraham Lincoln, it's good enough for you.

ETHEL:

Oh, don't drag in your boyhood pals, Fred.

The Facts of Life

LUCY:

What's Eve Whitney got that we haven't got? Nothing. We've got just as much as she's got only lots more.

ETHEL:

Yeah, but the lots more is in all the wrong places.

RICKY:

Look, all I know is that Columbus discovered Ohio in 1776.

RICKY:

But that's blackmail.

LUCY:

Oh, I wouldn't call it that.

RICKY:

But that's what it is.

LUCY:

I know, but let's not call it that.

LUCY:

He has to dance with a hundred young college girls. Can you think of anything worse than that?

FRED:

Yeah, I can think of a couple of things.

LUCY:
There's no reason why wives can't
be just as glamorous as other women.
After all, we were women once ourselves.

LUCY:
It's not the gift that counts.

It's the lack of thought behind it.

LUCY:
Some people are men and some people are women. They're made that way so they can dance together.

FRED:
Now, honey bunch, is that any way for you to talk to your apple dumpling?

ETHEL:
Fred, what's the matter with you?

FRED:
Nothing, sweetheart. It's just this ocean voyage . . . the sea air . . . you and I together. It just gets me.

ETHEL:
Yeah, in the head!

RICKY:

You know something, Lucy?

LUCY:

What?

RICKY:

Being married to you is not easy—

LUCY:

NO . . .

RICKY:

But it sure is
a lot of fun!